*Life in
Tudor Times*

✥

Life in a
Tudor Town

Jane Shuter

Heinemann

First published in Great Britain by Heinemann Library
an imprint of Heinemann Publishers (Oxford) Ltd
Halley Court, Jordan Hill, Oxford OX2 8EJ

MADRID ATHENS PARIS
FLORENCE PRAGUE WARSAW
PORTSMOUTH NH CHICAGO SAO PAULO
SINGAPORE TOKYO MELBOURNE AUKLAND
IBADAN GABORONE JOHANNESBURG

Designed by Ron Kamen, Green Door Design, Basingstoke, Hampshire
Printed in Spain by Mateu Cromo Artes Graficas SA

99 98 97 96 95
10 9 8 7 6 5 4 3 2 1

ISBN 0 431 06751 1 [HB]

99 98 97 96 95
10 9 8 7 6 5 4 3 2 1

ISBN 0 431 06773 2 [PB]

British Library Cataloguing in Publication Data
Heinemann Our World Topic Books. - Life in Tudor Times. - Life in a Tudor Town
I. Shuter, Jane
942.05

Acknowledgements
The Publishers would like to thank the following for permission to reproduce photographs:
British Library: p. 5C, p. 16A
The Governing Body, Christ Church, Oxford: p. 20B
Courtesty of St Martin's Church Canterbury, photo by C M Dixon: p. 11A
Fitzwilliam Museum, Cambridge/Bridgeman Art Library: p. 22B
Fotomas Index: p. 28A, p. 29B
Giraudon/Bridgeman Art Library: p. 25B
Glasgow University/Bridgeman Art Library: p. 6/7, 8/9
Hulton Deutsch: p. 29B
Mansell Collection: p. 17C
Mary Evans Picture Library: p. 26A
Michael Jenner/Robert Harding Picture Library: p. 19B
Museum of London: p. 13C
Peter Jackson/Museum of London: p. 18A (HOUSE DRAWING)
Science and Society Picture Library: p. 27B
Shakespeare's Birthday Trust: p. 12A
Stedelijk Museum de Lakenhal, Leiden, Holland: p. 15C

Cover photograph © Glasgow University/Bridgeman Art Library

Our thanks to Mike Mullett of the University of Lancaster for his comments in the preparation of this book.

Money
12 pence (d) in a shilling (s)
20 shillings (s) in a pound (£)

Contents

1 How Tudor towns grew

Did all towns grow?

When we talk about the size of towns we mean the number of people living in them. Many towns doubled in size during Tudor times, some grew even more. London was almost four times bigger in 1603 than in 1485. But not all towns grew. Some got smaller. The towns that grew did so mostly because they had a lot of **trade**. A lot of people moved into them, all looking for work.

Why move to towns?

Foreign workers came, hoping to make a better life for themselves in Britain than in their own country. They often brought skills, like making cloth or glass, that were needed in the towns. Some townspeople welcomed foreign workers. Others did not. They thought that the newcomers were taking jobs that they should have.

People from the countryside around the towns came hoping to find work. Some of them had lost their jobs in the country and had been thrown out of their houses, which were part of the payment for the job. These people, mostly farmworkers, did not have useful skills. Many of them did not find any work, but stayed in the town living as best they could, even if it meant **begging** and stealing.

Source A

Norwich, 21 August 1567

Dear wife,

   You would never believe how friendly the people are here. Come with half our property and see for yourself. Do not be anxious. There is no hatred for our people here, no matter what we have heard. Bring two little wooden dishes to make butter, for all our people here make their own, as the English use mostly pig fat.

A letter from Claus van Wervkin, a hat-maker from Ypres (now in modern Belgium), to his wife. Many foreign workers came to Britain alone at first, to see what it was like. Then they sent for their families.

Source B

   When farm workers and their families are turned out of their homes what can they do? They sell what little they possess for whatever they can get and wander about in search of work till they have spent all they have. What can they do then but steal, and justly be hanged for it, or go begging?

From *Utopia*, written by Sir Thomas More in 1516. Sir Thomas More was an important man who was adviser to Henry VIII until he was executed for his religious beliefs.

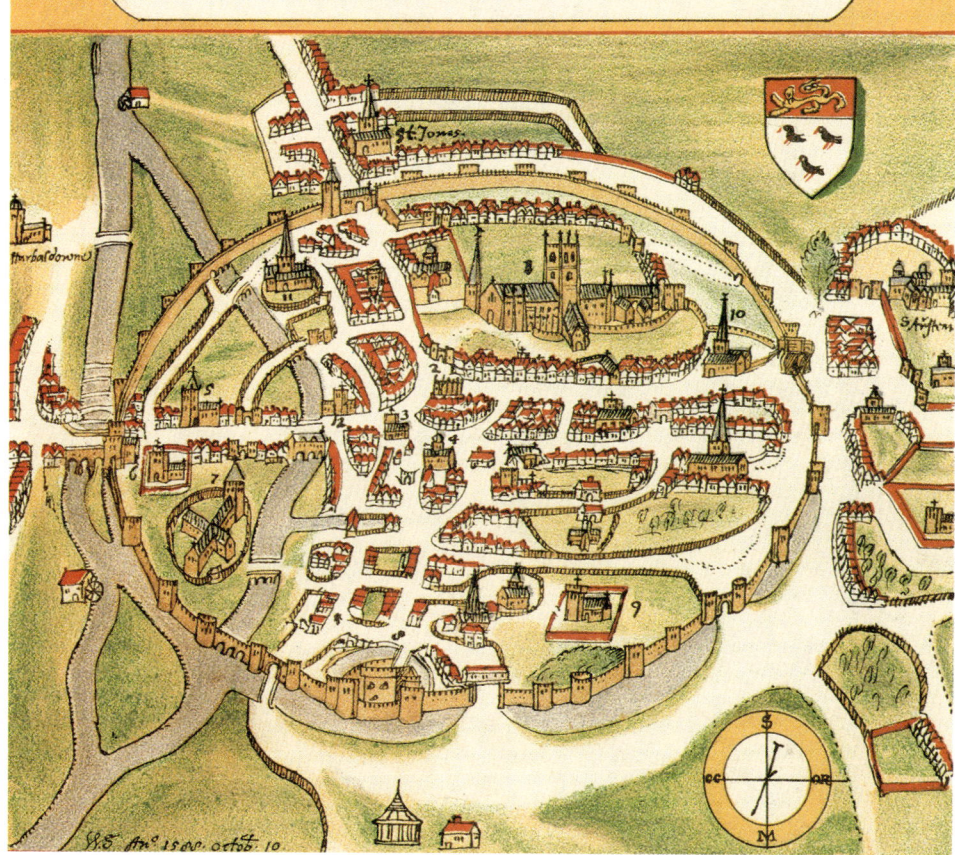

CANTERBVRY.

The city of Canterbury in Kent. This engraving was made in 1600. Building has already begun outside the city walls. The biggest buildings are the cathedral and the churches.

Most towns and cities were built by a river. There is a watermill for grinding corn on the river just outside the city wall on the left of the picture.

How some Tudor towns grew

Town	1520	1603
London	50,000	200,000
Norwich	12,000	15,000
Bristol	10,000	12,000
York	8,000	11,000
Exeter	8,000	9,000
Leicester	3,000	3,500
Warwick	2,000	3,000

The towns above are some of the largest. Most towns had between 1,000 and 1,500 people in them.

Which towns grew the fastest?

London was the fastest growing city. People were drawn to London because it was a busy **port** for trade with other countries. It also had a lot of **industries** in and around the city.

The towns that grew fastest were new towns set up to specialize in one craft. Workers setting up a new cloth industry in Norwich used the latest methods and so produced better cloth, faster than workers in older cloth-making towns like Coventry.

2 London

London, 1560.

Even though London was the biggest city in Britain, it would not take a person long to walk from the middle of the city to the countryside. Many houses, even in the town centre, had their own gardens.

An engraving in
German atlas.

The Spitel fields

The Towre

Look for the Tower of London (*The Towre*), Westminster (*West Muster*) and the bear baiting pit (*The Beare bayting*). There is only one bridge over the river. People hired small boats to get across.

The map on pages 6–7 was first printed in a German atlas in 1572. The map-maker used drawings made in 1560. It tells us a lot about sixteenth century London. The boxes on this page are close-ups of parts of the big map. In some boxes there are quotations from *A Survey of London*, written in 1598 by John Stowe. It was the first history of the city and talks about every street. It also lists some of the monuments in London's many churches. The quotes from Stowe are in *italics*.

Source A

The country is governed from London. This city is on the River Thames, which is deep and wide enough for ships of any size. It is second only to Venice as a trade centre. Its harbour is so thick with masts and sails that it is like a forest. Many of the streets are dark and narrow. But it has many fine buildings.

A description of London written by Barron Waldstein, an Austrian, who visited in 1600. A visit to London was part of the 'Grand Tour' made by many rich, young, European men.

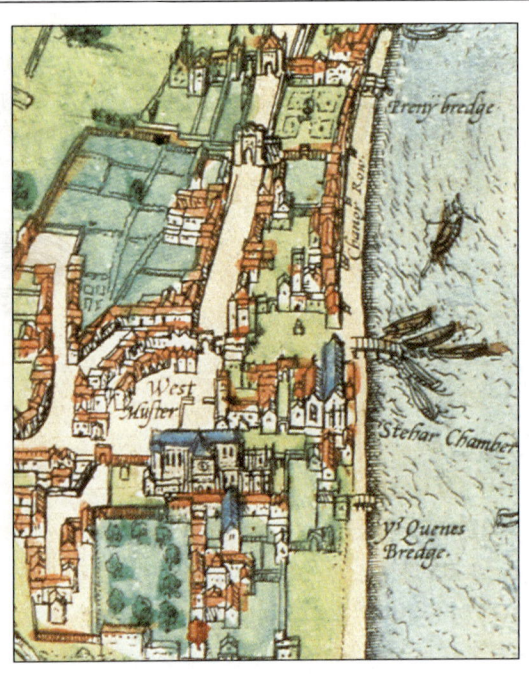

Westminster
The King, his advisers and parliament ran the country from Westminster. The royal palaces of Westminster and Whitehall were here. The kings and queens of England were crowned and buried in Westminster Abbey. This is the big building under the words 'West Muster'. Parliament met in the palace

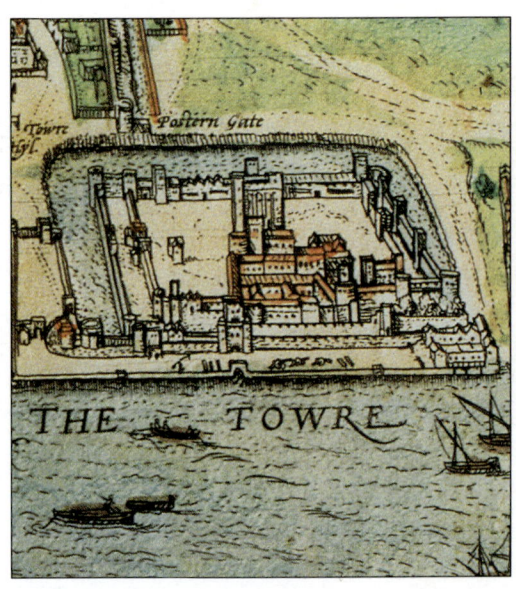

The Tower of London
The Tower of London was on the edge of the city. Stowe made a list of its uses. *This tower is a castle to defend or command the city. It is also a royal palace. It is a prison for the most dangerous criminals. They made all the coins in the country here. They keep a lot of armour and weapons here. The royal family keep their money and jewels here. The royal courts at Westminster keep their records here.*

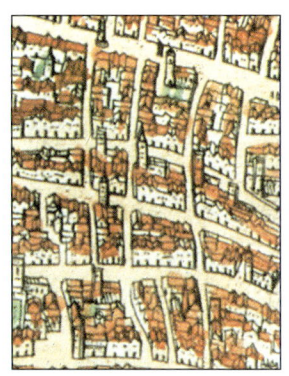

The city centre

The houses in this part of the city were crowded together. They were wooden with tiled or thatched roofs. **Craftworkers** lived in many of them. They had shops on the ground floor, facing the street, and workshops behind them. The people lived on the first floor. There are six churches in this small area. Everyone went to church, so they needed lots of them. The churches were built from stone.

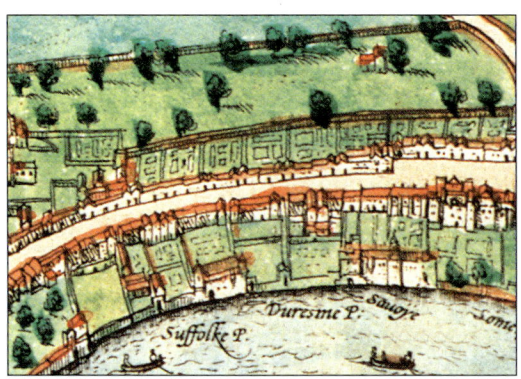

The Strand

The road that runs across the picture is the Strand. The houses that were on the riverside were very big. Their gardens led down to the river. Only very rich and important noble families lived in these houses. The houses on the other side of the Strand were smaller. They were close together and had smaller gardens. But people who lived in them were still quite rich.

Southwark

Southwark was on the other side of the river from the city. It was a place where people often went for entertainment. *There are two bear gardens, one old and one new. Bears, bull and other animals are kept there to be* **baited***. Dogs are also kept and fed, to bait them. Those who go to watch, sit or stand in galleries that go all around the baiting pit.*

London Bridge

There was only one bridge in London. *It has twenty stone arches some sixty feet high and twenty feet apart. There are houses on both sides of the bridge.* Ships went through the arches up and down the river, with the tide. People often moved around London by river. Many streets had steps down to the river.

3 Thomas Stoughton, 1535–91

Thomas Stoughton lived in or near Canterbury, in Kent, all his life. He owned three inns in the town and also **rented** out houses and land in the town and villages nearby. Thomas married a local girl, Jane Omer, who died before him. He did not marry again. He had three daughters who married local **gentlemen**. We know about Stoughton because he made a **will** in 1591 that divided up all his **property**. The will still exists.

Stoughton was one of the better-off townsmen of Canterbury. He inherited land and houses from his father and, as he made more money, bought more land and houses to rent out. Most of the land left in his will was in Kent. Like many people, Stoughton did his business in the town but lived in a bigger house with more land in a nearby village.

Stoughton's will

The will is a **legal** document, so it is business-like rather than chatty. But you can still work out things about the family. Stoughton divided up his things between his family, friends and servants. His will lists everything, even down to his twelfth best chest. Most people did this so that there would be no mistake or argument. But Thomas must have felt his family was more likely than most to argue because he added a clause which said that people who argued about the will would get nothing at all.

Property Stoughton owned
Inns in Canterbury – The Three Kings, The Fleur de Lys and The Bull. Houses and land in Ash, Canterbury, Sandwich and nearby villages. Some land to keep sheep on further away, but still in Kent. Houses and land in Surrey left by his father.

Money left to family
His two eldest grand-daughters were to have £200 at eighteen or as soon as they married. The other four grand-daughters were to have £100 each when they were twenty-one or as soon as they married. He left £100 to any girls born after his death.

Stoughton also left money to be paid twice yearly to various members of the family, as well as leaving them rents from properties he owned. His servants, and his children's servants, were left clothes, possessions and money ranging from a few shillings to £10.

Things Stoughton owned
Pewter, brass and silver household goods. Kitchen equipment. Lots of furniture, bedding and clothes. The things he owned in the inns were left in them, not listed separately.

Money for the Poor
£5 to buy goods and to provide work for the poor in St Martin's parish. 20s to the poor of Ash parish. 20s to the poor of St Paul's parish.

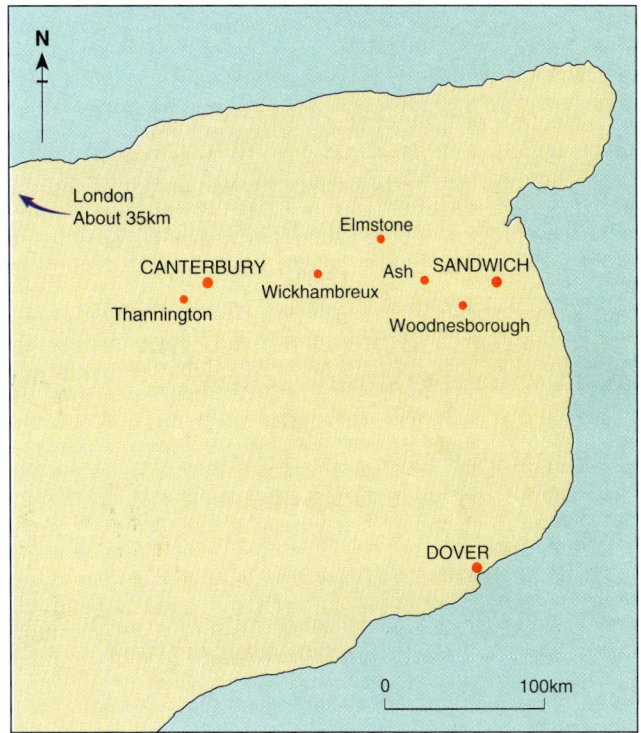

Source A

The brass memorial to Thomas Stoughton, in the Church of St Martin, Canterbury.

Source B

To my son-in-law's kitchen boy, I give 20 shillings.

To my brother, Joel, I give my best gown, my 2 best jackets, my best stockings, 2 best shirts and my best hat.

I give to Edward Fuller, my sister's son, 2 best brass pots, 2 pans, 6 wooden plates, 6 pewter dishes, 6 pewter plates, 6 tablecloths, 36 napkins, 6 pairs of sheets, bedding, 2 candlesticks and £10 in money.

I give to Jzanna Newman, my sister Omer's daughter, my worst coverlet, 40 shillings and two old feather mattresses.

I give to Elinor Wilde, my daughter's daughter, my wife's wedding ring.

Part of Thomas Stoughton's will.

This map shows the part of Kent where Thomas Stoughton lived.

4 Growing up

Babies

Many of the babies born in towns were likely to die at or soon after birth. Towns were regularly hit by **infectious diseases**. Babies were most likely to catch these diseases and die from them. Babies who lived were expected to be quiet and still. They were **swaddled** (wrapped in cloths like an Egyptian mummy) for the first months of their lives. This kept them still and quiet. Tudor books on childcare said this made sure their arms and legs grew straight.

Going to school

Children were educated differently, depending on what they were expected to do when they grew up. Some families believed girls should be educated, but most families educated boys to work and girls to marry. So, most girls were taught how to run a home by their mothers, or by the women of the house they were sent to live in. Towns offered a wide choice of schools to parents who could pay. Some boys, whose parents were the richest in the town, were taught at home by tutors. But other boys, whose parents could afford to send them, went to local **grammar schools**. Grammar schools taught Latin, Greek and mathematics. Ordinary local schools taught reading and writing, in English, to children whose parents could not afford grammar school fees. The sons of the better-off townspeople went from school to university, then to the Inns of Court in London (which taught law).

Source A

An early baby walker. The baby was put into the iron hoop to practise walking. Babies in baby walkers could be in the kitchen without fear of falling into the fire.

Learning a craft

People with skilled jobs were called **craftworkers**. The children of craftworkers often followed their parents into the same craft. They became **apprentices**. Their parents paid for them to learn a craft (like baking or making shoes) from another craftworker.

Apprentices lived with their master (the person they were apprenticed to) and worked for them for about five years. They were taught their craft and provided with food, clothes and lodgings. Some girls also learned craft skills and some women did run businesses. Other girls stayed at home and learned how to run a home until they were married. Some families sent their girls to live in other families to learn this.

Source **B**

John Hubbard binds himself to William Tebb, master baker, for 7 years as an apprentice and 1 year as a **journeyman**. As an apprentice he will be given 8d a year and 6d a week as a journeyman. Tebb will feed him and provide his clothes while he is an apprentice, and teach him the craft of baking. Hubbard will not gamble, sell anything for his own profit, or marry without permission.

From an agreement made between a baker and his apprentice in 1531. A journeyman was a trained apprentice.

Source **C**

Later sixteenth century child's jerkin (jacket). Children's clothes were the same style as adult clothes. Very few clothes have survived and most of the information we have about them comes from paintings made at the time.

5 Working in towns

Work in towns varied, depending on how rich and important the townspeople were. A rich **merchant** spent his day running the business. If he lived in London he spent a lot of his time at the newly built **Royal Exchange**, the centre of **trade**. If he lived in a smaller town he travelled to and from his trading **port**.

Working at a craft

Men and women who were **craftworkers** ran their businesses from home. In most towns the crafts were organized into **guilds**. Anyone who wanted to be a **weaver** had to pay to join the weavers' guild. If they could not afford to join they were not allowed to work in that town. Craftworkers often had houses with a shop in the downstairs room that faced the street. This room had a big wooden flap that was let down to make a counter out onto the street. The room at the back was the workshop. The master and his family lived in the upstairs rooms. Servants and **apprentices** slept in the attics or in the shop and workrooms.

Other townspeople had work that took them into the streets. There were water-sellers, who walked the streets with water from the river or local wells. There were people who sold pies or fruit or flowers from baskets that they carried round the streets. There were people who went from house to house with washing. Lastly there were the beggars, who wandered the streets asking for money for their next meal.

Market day

Not everyone lived and worked in the town all the time. Many towns had days when **markets** were held there. People came on market day from the local countryside, as well as the town, to buy and to sell. Farmers' wives came to sell any eggs, milk and other things they had to spare. Farmers came to sell sheep and cows. There were also people who made their living by following markets from town to town, selling things or offering to cut hair, trim beards, or pull out sore teeth.

Source A

No craft guild in the town of Oxford, or in the suburbs of Oxford, shall charge anyone who wishes to become a brother of their craft more than 20 shillings to join the guild.

A rule made by Oxford town council in November 1561. Guilds often tried to charge a lot of money to join, so that only better-off craftworkers could afford to trade in the town.

Source B

The bakers in this market bake bread that is not the weight set down by law.

The brewers Edward Pye, Widow Gaywood and some others brew beer that is not **wholesome,** and do not have someone to taste it first as they should.

The **fishmongers** here do not keep their fish freshly watered.

Inspectors visited the markets to make sure that the rules about what people could sell were being kept. The local law court fined people who broke the rules. This is part of a list of rules broken in Norwich in 1564.

Source C

Women spinning cloth in Leiden, in Holland, in the sixteenth century. They are using the latest machinery. There were a lot of women who worked at home in various crafts. Women's work was important to towns, but they were not always allowed to join guilds, and had no say in running the guilds or the town.

6 Marriage and family life

Townspeople married when they could afford to do so. The better-off **merchants** and **craftworkers** married off their children in their early twenties. Parents did not always choose who their children married, but children were expected to marry into families that were as well-off, or better-off, than their own. Parents often said that, if their children married people they disapproved of, they would leave the children nothing in their **wills**.

Forbidden to marry

Craftworkers who were learning a **trade** as **apprentices** married much later in life, often not until they were in their late twenties. They were forbidden by law to marry without the agreement of their masters. Masters very rarely agreed to marriages. So craftworkers often did not marry until they had set up in trade on their own.

Source B

The English show little affection to their children. When they are seven years old their parents put them out to hard **service**, in the houses of other people, for seven to nine years. They then take in the children of others. Everyone, even the rich, does this. They say it is so their children learn manners or, in the case of apprentices, a trade. I think it is because they can be less kind to the children of others.

Written by an Italian who visited England in the early sixteenth century. He wrote a book about his travels which was printed in Italy.

Source A

This sixteenth century Tudor print, which was used to decorate a song sheet, shows a family having dinner together. The family ate together. Servants, apprentices and other members of the household ate separately.

Life in a household

Better-off families lived as part of a **household**. A household was the family, servants, apprentices, relatives, even friends. Everyone from the master of the house and his family to the kitchen boy who scrubbed the floors was included.

Everyone in a household had **rights** that they could ask of the others. They all had **duties** to the others, too. The master had the right to obedience from everyone. But he had the biggest responsibility too. He was expected to make sure that everyone in his household was well fed and cared for. He also had to train his apprentices, educate his children and care for any relatives who needed his help.

This Tudor print comes from a book of Psalms (verses from the Bible) printed in 1563. It shows a father explaining the meaning of a Psalm to his family.

7 Houses and homes

Not all town houses were the same. There were a few big, well-built houses, with many rooms, where the better-off people lived. There were many more smaller houses, all squeezed together, often with a room that faced the street as a shop. These houses had several rooms, but there were often lots of people living in them. There was the owner, his wife and children (maybe grandchildren too), servants and any **apprentices** who worked for him.

The worst houses were in the poorer parts of town. Many were near noisy or smelly craft workshops (like leather **tanneries**).

These houses were often badly made and badly looked after. They were **rented**, and their owners crammed them full of people. This was where **diseases** and fires were most likely to break out, and spread quickly.

Fire

Fire was a big risk in Tudor times, because most houses were made of wood and roofed with straw. The main way of fighting fire was to carry water in buckets from the river. This was slow and made it hard to put out a fire that had got a good hold.

Plans of town houses in London, taken from drawings made in 1612, and an artist's idea of what they would have looked like.

Source A

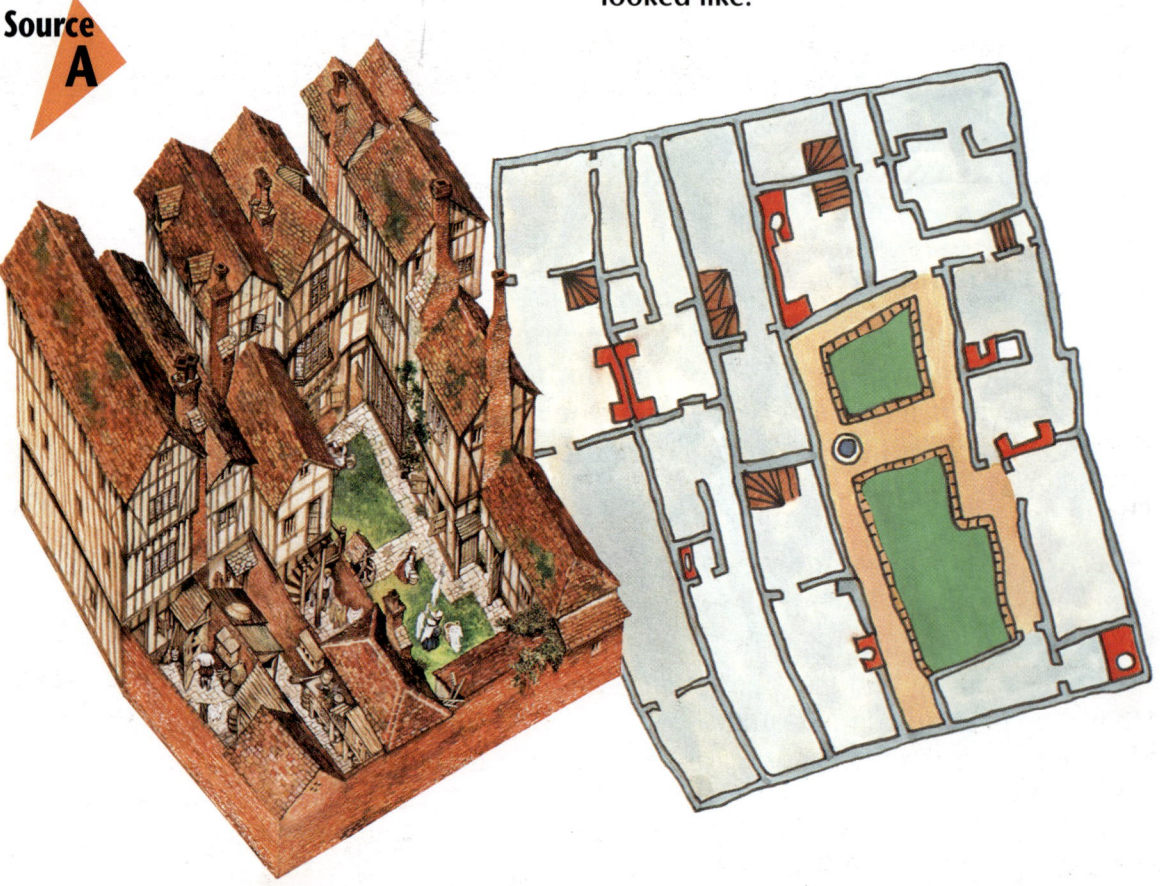

Houses in towns were built close together. This is a picture of sixteenth century houses still standing in Tewkesbury, Gloucester. Notice how the first floor of the house on the right juts out over the street. In some towns the streets were so narrow that people on the first floors of houses that faced each other could lean out of their windows and touch each other.

Possessions

The sort of house people lived in depended on how well off they were. Money also affected how comfortable they could make their homes. Better-off townspeople could afford basins, bowls and plates made out of brass, **pewter** or silver. They could buy carved wooden furniture. They had plenty of bedding and chests (wooden boxes) to keep them in. They could have **tapestries** on the walls and glass in the windows. We know all this from reading their **wills**. Poor people, living in crowded, rented rooms, had far fewer possessions. Some of them left wills that showed they only had a few tools, a couple of stools and a mattress. Some of them had nothing to leave, so did not make wills at all.

Source C

First they make a frame of wood, joined by wooden pegs. Between the layers of wood they put bricks. The houses have many windows, filled with clear glass. The roofs have a steep slope, and are covered in lead more often than tile. Inside, houses have beautiful wooden carvings. They have tapestries on the walls. The floors are covered in straw. They have tin dishes full of flowers and sweet smelling herbs by the windows.

A description of houses in London, written in 1562 by Alessandro Magno, an Italian visitor.

8 Shopping

Town shops sold all sorts of things, depending on the size of the town. A small town would have butchers, bakers, **fishmongers**, shoe and boot-makers as well as **apothecaries**, (selling medicines, herbs and spices), and drapers selling cloth. These shops were likely all to be in the same area of the town. Many towns today still have streets called 'Butchers' Row' or 'Fish Street' that tell you what **trades** there were in that area. Larger towns would have more of all of these shops and other shops which sold things like gold and silver **plate** and jewellery. London, of course, had the most shops with the widest range of goods.

London also had several **markets**. Markets were another way townspeople could shop, especially for food. Farmers' wives brought the extra food that they produced each week.

Source A

Lately many people have started to buy things like eggs, butter, cheese, chickens, pigs and bacon in their local market and then send their wives to other markets to sell them for more, especially to London, where all things cost more. This is despite all rules that there are against this.

Written in 1577, by William Harrison, in his book called *A Description of England*.

Source B

A butcher's shop, painted by Annibale Carracci in the sixteenth century. Notice the wooden flap that has been folded down to become the counter.

There are few towns that do not have a weekly market that sells all a person needs for the week. There are rules about the weight of bread and the freshness of corn and other things, yet people are still cheated, for **magistrates** do not always make sure the rules are obeyed.

Written in 1577, by William Harrison, in his book, *A Description of England*.

Antwerp market, painted in the later sixteenth century by an unknown artist. Antwerp is in modern Belgium. Some town markets, like this one, sold anything and everything. Others sold particular things, like sheep or cattle. Some markets had hiring **fairs**, were where people went to get hired as house servants or farmworkers.

9 Entertainment

Towns provided lots of entertainment. People could go to the inns and **taverns** and eat, drink and play cards and gamble. They could watch bear and bull **baiting** or **cock-fighting**. Some towns had special buildings with pits for this. In smaller towns the nearest bit of open space was used. People could also watch plays. By the end of the period London had several theatres built for performances, but in most towns, plays were put on in the courtyards of inns or in any large space.

There were many wandering entertainers who called at towns, often at the same time as the town had a **fair** or **holiday**. These included people with performing animals (such as bears), acrobats, fire-eaters and jugglers (who often travelled together) and people who performed magic tricks.

People also entertained themselves at home by singing and playing musical instruments, playing with dice and cards and reading, often aloud.

Source B

Morris dancers, entertaining some Londoners, painted in 1620 by a Dutch artist. The river is the Thames and the building in the background is Richmond Palace.

Source A

Repairs to the bull baiting ring
A man who brought a serpent (snake) to the town
Martin the minstrel
The Turkish tumblers (acrobats)
The players (actors) from London
A blind minstrel

Some payments made by the town council for entertainments in Ipswich between 1570 and 1600.

10 Food and drink

Townspeople had a much wider choice of food and drink than people living in the country. On the other hand, they had to pay more for it. In some towns, especially London, the price of food was high, because there were a lot of people in the city who wanted to buy food and this pushed the price up.

Rich and poor

What people ate depended on what they could afford. Poor people managed on a diet of bread and cheese and kept a pot on the fire, full of vegetables and whatever else they could get – a piece of bacon or a pig's trotter or tail. They usually made their own beer, which was quite thin and watery. At the other end of the scale came the richer townspeople. They were often the town council (the people who ran the town) and gave **official** dinners. They ate a lot of meat and fish and pastries stuffed full of expensive sugar, currants and spices. They thought vegetables were less important, but ate parsnips, carrots, cabbage and turnips. Salads were becoming more popular. They drank wine.

In between, came the ordinary townspeople. The food they ate came somewhere in between, too. They ate a lot of bread and stews, but the stews often had meat in. They ate pastries and roasted meat on special occasions. Everyone ate fruit when it was in season.

Source A

Any good man feeding his family and friends should give them beef boiled and roasted, chicken, roast **venison** and pork, tongue, beef pies, goose, turkey and swan (if it can be got) roasted. With this serve cooked sallets (vegetables) if you wish. Be sure to have tarts made from fruit and custard.

Written by the English traveller, Gervaise Markham, in 1601.

Source B

A mid-sixteenth century painting of women in the kitchen of a town house. Notice the pan to catch the fat from the meat that is roasting on a spit. They are cooking much more meat than vegetables (which are in the basket by the door).

11 Health

Keeping healthy

Townspeople were more likely to catch **infectious diseases** than people who lived in the country. There were more people collected together into one place, so diseases spread more easily. People, including the butchers and **fishmongers**, threw their rubbish and **sewage** into the street or the river. They used the water from the river for cooking and brewing beer. Town councils tried to get people to keep the streets clean. They passed regulations (rules) about not throwing rubbish into the street. But this was what people had always done. It was hard to get them to stop. Some people who saw how polluted the rivers were, bought their water from water-sellers who said their water came from fresh springs. It was often taken from the river.

Care for the sick

In most towns sick people had a choice of treatment. In a village there was often just one old woman who knew about using herbs to cure diseases. In towns there were often several doctors, as well as old women and other people who would use magic to cure the sick. There were also **apothecaries**, like chemists today, who sold medicines and gave advice.

An apothecary's shop drawn in about 1510. Apothecaries mixed up drugs to make medicine for each customer. This is what the apprentice on the left is doing.

Source A

Sixteenth-century jars for storing medicine. These come from Italy, but English apothecaries used similar jars. Some medicines were bought from apothecaries. A person did not have to be a doctor to buy them. Some of the drugs doctors used, especially the herbal ones, worked very well. The herb used for headaches then is still used in asprin today.

Plague!

One of the most feared infectious diseases that swept through Tudor towns was the plague. It was spread by bites from fleas that came from the black rats that were everywhere, living in the walls of the houses and eating the rubbish in the streets.

People saw that plague was spread by some sort of contact. Some thought it was spread by breathing infected air. Others thought it was spread by touch, or by animals. They did not even think about the rats, or fleas. They were too much a part of everyday life to be noticed.

People did many of the right sorts of things to stop the plague. They tried to keep infected people away from others. They shut them up in their own homes, or in special buildings called 'plague houses'. Some towns ordered that all animals in the town should be killed. Almost all towns tried to keep the streets clean. People were told to keep away from the big pits that were dug to bury those who died from the plague. But the plague kept coming back. In some years there were only a few deaths. In other years hundreds of townspeople died, thousands in London.

12 Death

Many Tudor townspeople left money to set up schools or **almshouses** for the poor to live in, as a way to be remembered after their death. Others left money to the poor or to the church. We can find out a lot about townspeople by looking at the **wills** they made just before they died.

What wills can tell us

These wills carefully divided up the land and possessions of the person making the will. One of the most obvious things they tell us is how well-off the people were, and how many things they possessed. These things included **pewter**, silver and brass bowls, cups and plates; quilts and bedding; clothes and hats.

Wills also show us how the townspeople used their money. They often bought land or houses and **rented** them out, to make more money. Most of the better-off people had **property** that they rented out.

Wills also show us how people felt about women and their place in the world. Most young women who were left money could not have it until they were eighteen (or even twenty-one) unless they married. If they married, they got the money straight after the wedding. In most cases they then had to hand it over to their husband. Wills do seem to show that women, especially young women, were not seen as being able to handle their own money sensibly.

Wills and families

Wills can also show us what the people who made them felt about their families. Who did they leave their best things to? Who did they put in charge of carrying out the will? Who did they leave the third best quilt to? But we have to be very careful when we think about the things that were left in wills. The best things may have been left to the oldest – rather than the favourite – child. We also have to realize that something like the third best quilt was still a thing that was well worth having at the time, not an insult.

Source A

Avice Gibson, wife of Nicholas Gibson, grocer, in 1545 set up a free school in Radcliffe, near London, for sixty poor men's children. She also built almshouses for fourteen poor, old people, and whoever lived in these houses was to have 6s 8d a year for as long as they lived there.

From *The Survey of London* by John Stowe, written in 1598. This book was a detailed description of London, including the churches there and the charities that were set up.

An engraving made by Crispin de Passe in about 1585. It shows a rich man lying in bed, obviously just about to die.

Dying in peace?

The man in the picture was not left alone to die in peace.

There is a doctor taking his pulse. The doctor's assistant is showing the doctor a specimen of the man's urine.

The man's lawyer is sitting at the table in the foreground, writing out the man's will.

Many members of the family and animals are also in the room.

GLOSSARY

almshouse a house built for the poor to live in, usually without paying any rent

apothecary a shopkeeper who sells herbs, spices and medicine

apprentice a young boy who works for a master to learn a craft

bait to set dogs on to bulls and bears to fight and kill them

begging asking for money

cock-fighting making two cockerels fight each other

craftworker a person who has the skill of making something

disease sickness

duties things that you have to do for other people

fair Where people get together to trade things, like horses. Often there are entertainers and people selling food there too.

fishmonger a fish seller

foreign from a country different from your own

gentleman a man with an income of between £500 and £700 a year

grammar school A school for boys, paid for and run by local people, not the government. They taught mainly Latin and possibly Greek.

guild A town organization which runs a craft. Everyone with that skill has to pay to join the guild, or they cannot work in the town.

holiday A holy day. People did not have to work, but went to church instead.

household everyone who lives in a house, including the family and their servants, and the things in the house.

industry lots of people all working together to produce one thing

infectious easily spread from one person to another

journeyman a person who has been an apprentice to a craftworker, but who is not a guild member, and works for a craftworker rather than running his own business

legal to do with the laws of the country

magistrate the local person who makes sure that the law is carried out in that part of the country

market place where people from the countryside go to buy and sell things

Henry VII	Henry VIII
1485	1509

merchant a person who buys and sells things

official connected with people who are in charge of running things

pewter a mixture of tin and lead used to make plates and mugs

plate plates, cups, bowls, jugs etc. made out of silver or gold

port a place on the coast or a river with a harbour for ships to load and unload in

property things a person owns – land, money and possessions

rent To pay money to someone to use something. If a house is rented out, people live in it and pay the owner rent.

rights things you can expect other people to do for you

Royal Exchange a building in London, built in 1571, where merchants met to trade things and to talk about trading

service domestic work in someone else's home

sewage water and toilet contents

swaddle Wrap a baby up in strips of cloth, like an Egyptian mummy. Swaddling kept babies still and quiet, and was said to help their bones grow straight.

tannery a place where animal skins had the flesh scraped off and were soaked in urine to turn them into leather

tapestry a piece of cloth with a picture woven on to it

tavern a place where people could go and buy food and drink

trade buying and selling things (as used on page 4) or a skilled job or profession (as used on page 16)

venison the meat from a stag or a deer

weaver someone who takes wool and turns it into cloth, on a machine called a loom

wholesome safe to eat or drink

will a list that people make of what they want to happen to all their property (money, land and possessions) after they are dead

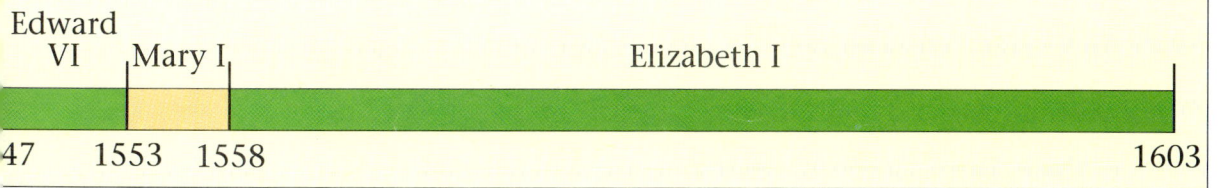

Edward VI | Mary I | Elizabeth I

47 1553 1558 1603

INDEX

Plain numbers (3) refer to the text. Bold numbers (**3**) refer to a source. Italic numbers (*3*) refer to a picture. Underlined numbers (<u>3</u>) refer to an information box.